KIWI AARDVARK LOOKS AT CLIMATE SCIENCE

Kiwi Aardvark looks at Climate Science

Temperature
average · winter · summer

KIWI AARDVARK

Kiwi Aardvark

What is Climate?

Climate is the average weather at a location, averaged over many years.

Climate is typically averaged over a period of 30 years.

Climate includes the average and variability of a number of meteorological or weather variables.

Some of the meteorological variables that are commonly measured are

- temperature
- humidity
- atmospheric pressure
- wind
- precipitation

The climate at a location is affected by its latitude, terrain, and altitude, as well as nearby water bodies and their currents.

Average Temperatures

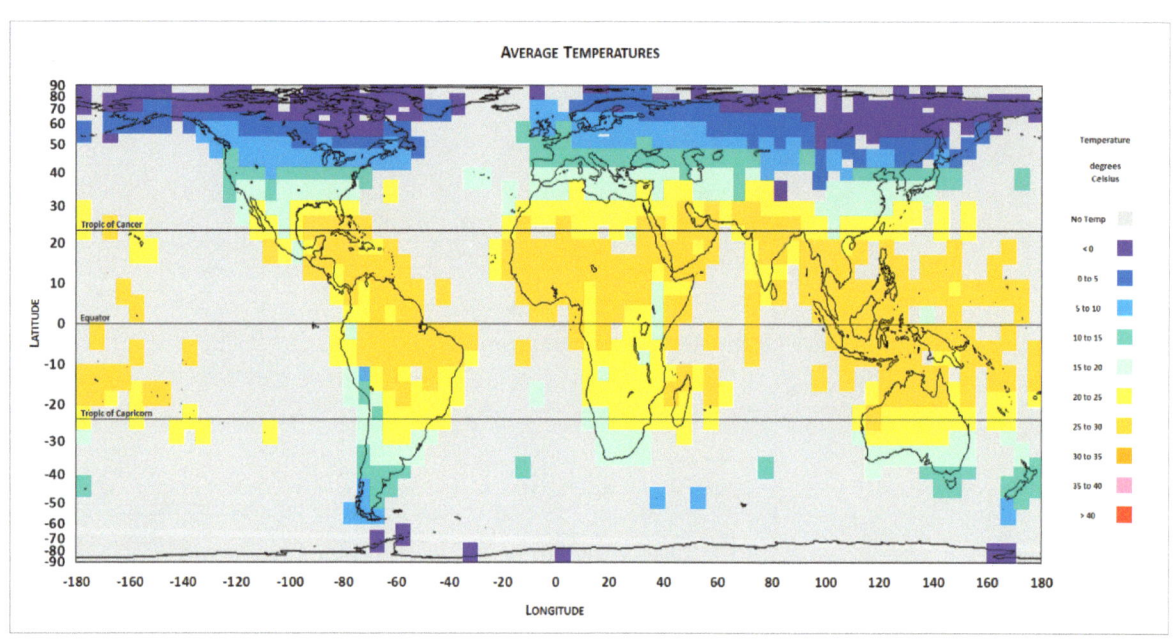

Things to do

- Find the location where you live on the temperature map

- What color is at that location?

- Look up the color in the Legend, to find the temperature range for that color

- Your average temperature is in that temperature range

Extra for experts

- Look on the temperature map to see which locations have an average temperature which is warmer than where you live

- Look on the temperature map to see which locations have an average temperature which is cooler than where you live

- Do you live in a location which is cold, cool, average, warm, or hot, compared to other locations?

Notes

The Earth in January

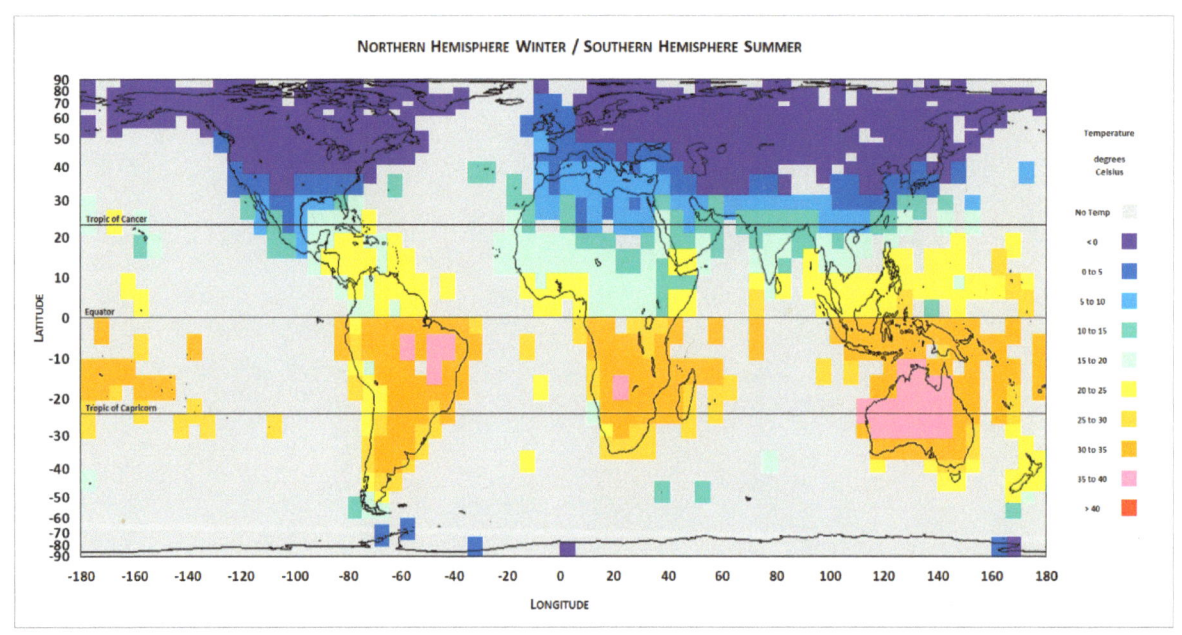

Things to do

- Find the location where you live on the temperature map

- What color is at that location?

- Look up the color in the Legend, to find the temperature range for that color

- Your January temperature is in that temperature range

- Is this temperature for summer or winter?

Extra for experts

- Look on the temperature map at the hemisphere that you live in. Which locations have a January temperature which is warmer than where you live?

- Look on the temperature map at the hemisphere that you live in. Which locations have a January temperature which is cooler than where you live?

- Do you live in a location which has a January temperature that is cold, cool, average, warm, or hot, compared to the other locations in the hemisphere that you live in?

Notes

The Earth in July

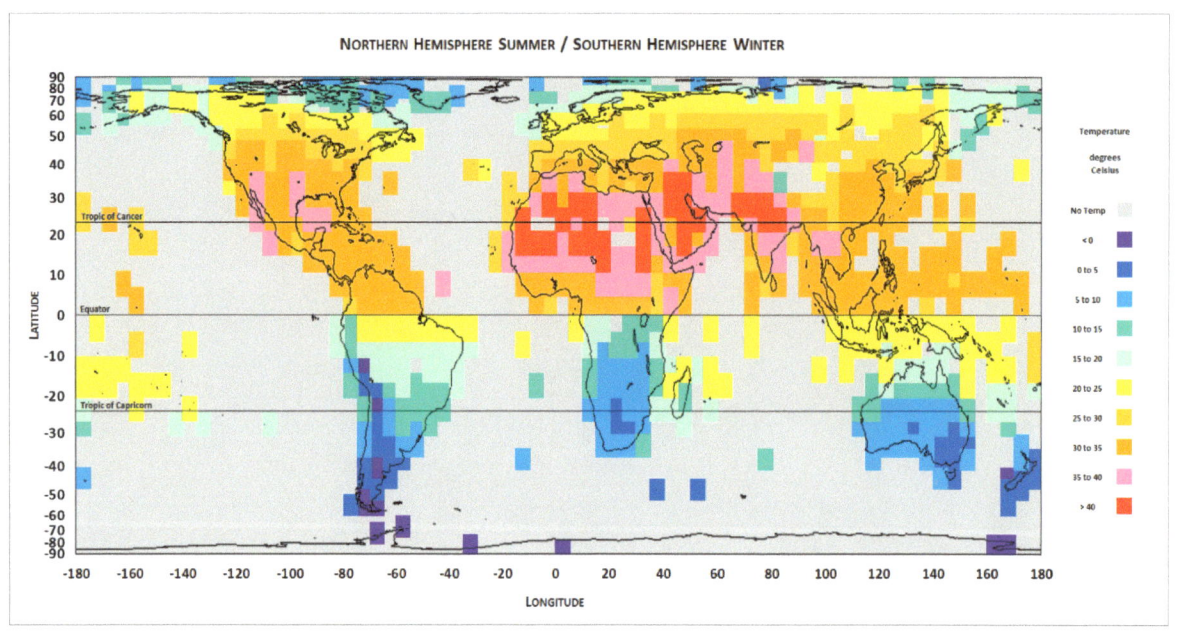

Things to do

- Find the location where you live on the temperature map

- What color is at that location?

- Look up the color in the Legend, to find the temperature range for that color

- Your July temperature is in that temperature range

- Is this temperature for summer or winter?

Extra for experts

- Look on the temperature map at the hemisphere that you live in. Which locations have a July temperature which is warmer than where you live?

- Look on the temperature map at the hemisphere that you live in. Which locations have a July temperature which is cooler than where you live?

- Do you live in a location which has a July temperature that is cold, cool, average, warm, or hot, compared to the other locations in the hemisphere that you live in?

Notes

Winter-Summer Temperature Difference

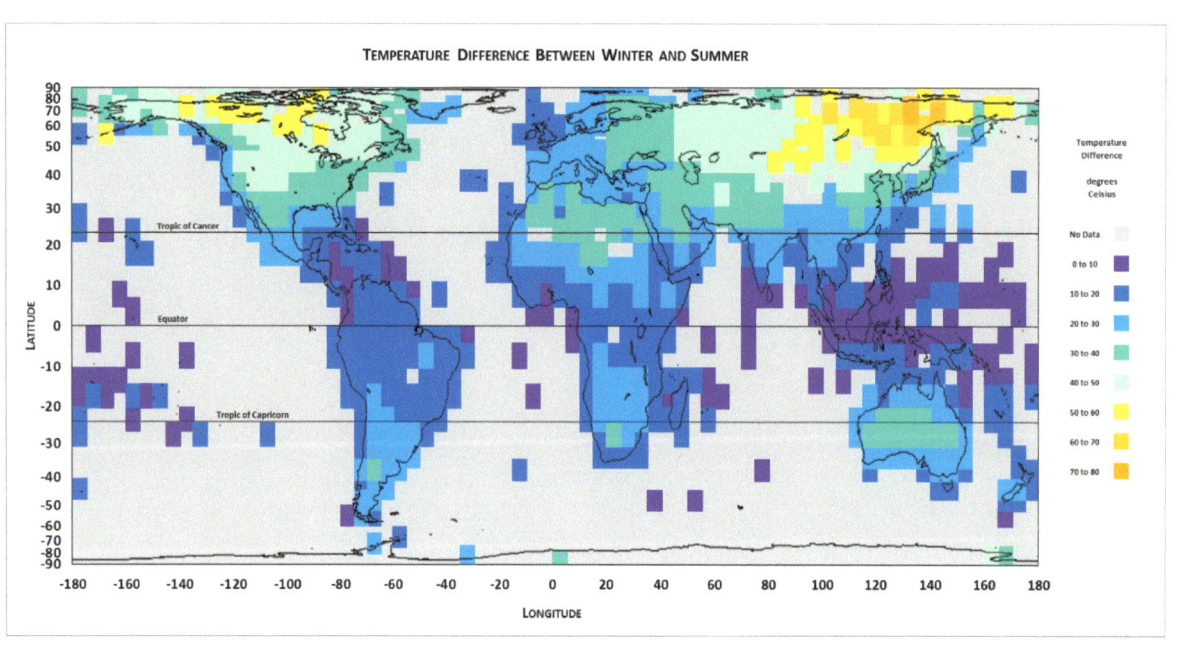

Things to do

- Find the location where you live on the temperature map

- What color is at that location?

- Look up the color in the Legend, to find the temperature range for that color

- Your winter-summer temperature difference is in that temperature range

Extra for experts

- Look on the temperature map to see which locations have a winter-summer temperature difference which is greater than where you live

- Look on the temperature map to see which locations have a winter-summer temperature difference which is less than where you live

- Do you live in a location which has a winter-summer temperature difference that is small, average, or large, compared to other locations?

Notes

Internet Information

Visit

Kiwi Aardvark

at

www.kiwi-aardvark.com

www.ingramcontent.com/pod-product-compliance
Lightning Source LLC
Chambersburg PA
CBHW041155290426
44108CB00002B/80